When Life Is A Barbed Wire Fence

Strategies to Harvest Better Living

VOLUME 1

When Life Is A Barbed Wire Fence

Strategies to Harvest Better Living

GREG WINSTON

VOLUME 1

When Life Is A Barbed Wire Fence

Strategies To Harvest Better Living

Requests for permission should be sent to:

Greg Winston
300 Queen Anne Ave., Ste. 339
Seattle, Washington 98109

Printed in the United States of America

ISBN: 0-9712539-0-0

Acknowledgments

Thank you Granddaddy. Thank you in ways that I can't fully explain. I hope that this book captures a small portion of what you have given to me. I know that without you my life would not have been as rich.

Marizol, I want to thank you for your love and spirit. Your support was daily with or without me having to ask for it. I love and appreciate you exactly 1000 times more than you can count.

I want to give a special thanks to Uncle Hainey, Renita, Aunt Cecil and Aunt Juanita. And Momma, the person I talked to most about Granddaddy, without you I would not have come this far. Most of what I am I owe to you … I love you.

Table of Contents

"The most important thing about a man is what he believes in the depth of his being. This is the thing that makes him what he is, the thing that organizes him and feeds him; the thing that keeps him going in the face of untoward circumstances; the thing that gives him resistance and drive."

– Hugh Stevenson Tigner

Introduction

It was the first family reunion I had attended in ten years. This one was being held in Little Rock, and July in Little Rock is wonderful... if you like it hot. Because I had spent a great deal of my youth in and around Little Rock, the trip from my new home in Seattle felt really exciting. It was an opportunity to see my entire family and, possibly, some old friends.[1]

Most of the visiting relatives came from Chicago, Indiana, and California. Since our numbers had mushroomed, we were making the downtown Doubletree "reunion headquarters." There we would have most of our planned activities—lunches, meetings, and a sit-down dinner with dancing afterward.

The reunion was great. For days, I visited with family, young and old, spent time with all the

---

1. Names have been changed to protect remaining family members.

"new" nieces and nephews, caught up on years of gossip…I had a wonderful time. Among my relatives were dentists, teachers, entrepreneurs, several homemakers, even a minister. We had plenty of occupational diversity. I couldn't help but think about how fortunate we were: a reunion of close to one hundred people, all successful, enjoying our time together.

On the second day of the reunion, I wandered down to the hotel lobby. As I walked around, I found myself near the bell captain's station. "Are you Greg Winston?" came a voice from behind me. I turned to see one of the bellmen smiling at me. "Remember me? I'm Larry Batchelor. I graduated the year after you did." "Yeah, I'm Greg," I said, trying to collect my thoughts and to place his face. Then it came to me. "Oh yeah! Batch, right?" That was the nickname we had pinned on him way back when.

We laughed, hugged each other, and immediately started to reminisce. We talked about the reunion, basketball, high school, and finally settled on people we both knew. Batch began to run down a list of guys. Some names I remembered right away and some I had to think about. As I listened I kept hearing the bad news: "died, in jail, on welfare, on drugs."

What a sobering conversation, I felt lucky just to be standing there. So many of the people I used to know were now dead or on very shaky terms. There were a few success stories, but not nearly what I had envisioned growing up. I thought, or maybe fantasized, that everyone who was a classmate of mine would be successful. If they were not exactly successful, certainly they would not be on drugs, or dead!

I left Batch, feeling saddened and wondering what had caused so many of my old friends to live out such tragedies. What was it that had saved me? And what was it that had enabled so many of my relatives to be so successful?

There are probably many reasons for the good fortune in my family, but one stands out. We had an extraordinary teacher—my grandfather, the man we all called Granddaddy. I began to question family members to learn more about how Granddaddy had affected them. Soon, I began to realize something mind-boggling. The relatives who seemed to know the most about Granddaddy were also the relatives who seemed to enjoy the most success. Success in business, success with their spouses, success with their kids; they seemed to succeed at whatever they tried.

Hard work was a religion with my granddaddy, and he worked God and learning into everything that was hard. I thought about how he had affected me, directly. I didn't realize it at the time, but my greatest lessons in life came from summer visits to my granddaddy's farm. His given name was General, which seems perfect for a man who led a family of 13. His surname was Cook, and he lived in the small town of Varner, Arkansas. In his time, he had accumulated up to 120 acres of land. He owned cows, horses, chickens, hunting dogs, pigs, and a prosperous farming business. More importantly, he earned the respect and trust of most of the people in that town.

My parents divorced when I was six, so I began my growing up without a father…without a male role model. The year I turned nine, though, my granddaddy got my attention. By today's standards his body type would be called athletic. Tall and lean with board-straight posture, he never knew a fat day in his life. He was wealthy in spirit as well as dollars, well dressed, admired by everyone, and the best storyteller I have ever heard. Perhaps these accomplishments will sound more impressive if I add that my granddaddy was a black farmer in the deepest regions of rural Arkansas. What's more, he achieved most of his success in and around the great depression.

As a child, I saw poverty all around me. I grew up in the ghettos of Gary, Indiana and Arkansas, where doing without was the rule rather than the exception. There was darkness living in the city; you could see it, and sometimes you could touch it. Life at my granddaddy's did not have the same negative overtone. It was only when I visited my granddaddy that I saw what real success looked like. Everything was plentiful, people loved him, and he never seemed to worry about not having enough of anything.

I soon became attached to granddaddy. We went everywhere together. If he worked, I worked. If he prayed, I prayed. If it was time for a haircut, we both got a trim. I remember asking him to buy me khaki pants and shirts like the ones he wore, and he did. But the most important things I tried to imitate were the stories and life lessons he shared with me.

He was a superb teacher who had only a third grade education. What he taught did not come from books, but from his own experience and observation. I shudder to think what my life might be like without the education he gave me. It taught me nothing less than how to work and how to live. I have replayed his advice over and over again, thankful that I listened. If I could have a single wish, it would be to sit and talk with him once more. Now that I have grown, I'm convinced I would ask better questions and naturally receive new insights from him.

Perhaps you, too, had someone in your life who advised you. Someone who spoke from experience, and gave you the benefit of their life lessons. If so, you are fortunate, and these stories may bring back some fond memories. If not, please feel free to "borrow" my granddaddy. It gives me great pleasure to share some of his wisdom with you.

Henry Cook "Great-Granddaddy"

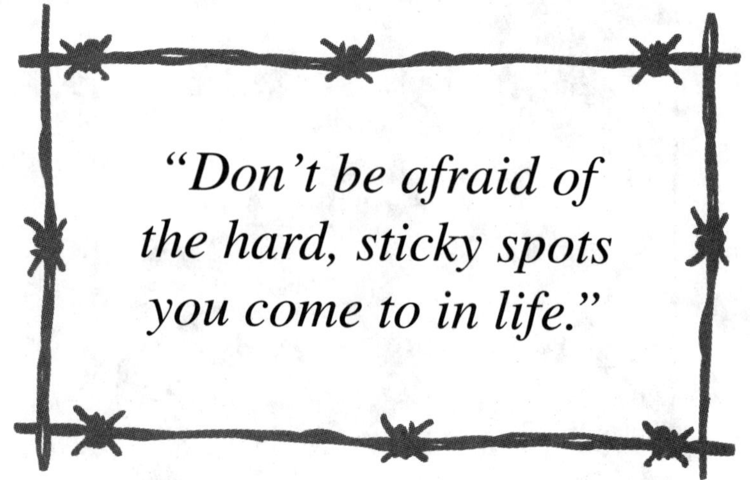
*"Don't be afraid of
the hard, sticky spots
you come to in life."*

Chapter 1

Life Is a Barbed Wire Fence

Granddaddy's farm was adjacent to an impressive farming machine called the Arkansas State Prison. One day, when the inmates were working close to his property, I sat and stared at them for a long time, stunned by their ability to work. You could hear and see them coming from a half-mile away. The prison guards rode on horseback and carried rifles, while the inmates, dressed all in white, jogged and chanted in time as they hurried to the day's work. A cloud of dust followed their progress toward the cotton fields. When they arrived at the field, they lined up single file, looking out impassively across the waves of Arkansas heat, waiting for the signal to begin.

After the signal was given, all you could hear were the rhythmic, almost musical, hacking sounds of prisoners chopping cotton and chanting as one. They worked hard and fast, ignoring the dust that had followed them to the field and was now following them as they moved along the rows of cotton plants. It didn't happen often, but when an inmate fell behind, he was immediately pulled from the field. Guards would throw him down on the hot, dusty road and beat him with a strap that looked like it was as long as the guard was tall. After five, six, sometimes seven lashes with the strap, the prisoner broke his stoic silence and cried out. Some cried for help, some cried for mercy, but all who were lashed eventually cried like children. It made my mouth dry and my heart pound.

Just then, Granddaddy's truck pulled up, I rushed to meet him, full of fearful questions. Why were those men in prison? What did you have to do to be put in prison? More importantly, what did you have to do to stay *out* of prison?

As usual, he found my curiosity amusing enough to make him smile. "By hammers, son," he said. "You're soon going to see that life is just like that barbed wire fencing holding the cows inside that pasture."

I pondered the idea of my life as a fence made of barbed wire, not liking it much. Just then, the work detail was called to a halt and the inmates got back into line. As they jogged toward the prison, Granddaddy continued his thought.

"Those prisoners had some problems, some sharp, sticky spots in their lives, just like the barbs in that wire fence. But because they didn't take care of them the way they should have, or because they tried to ignore them, the sticky spots caught them up, and they had to go to prison for a time." He patted my shoulder. "Son, don't ever be afraid of the hard, sticky spots you come to in life. You want to get very good at handling them instead of turning away from them. Then you can get back to enjoying the nice, smooth parts."

The most obvious application of the "Barbed Wire" theory happened when I worked for the CBS television affiliate in Seattle, Washington. My closest friend at the time was a former professional baseball player, Darrell Edwards. Darrell had recently been cut by the Orioles and had to go back to normal employment. He settled on a job as a clothing representative. As he traveled through the Northwest selling clothes, he saw his job as increasingly boring and mundane.

One day, while working at the television station, I received a phone call from Darrell. He was in the lobby and asked that I come down to talk to him. "If you give me $5,000, I can turn it into $20,000 by this weekend," he said, without preamble. "First of all, I don't have $5,000 in cash to lose, and second, why would I just hand it over to you?" I quickly responded.

Darrell paused for a second, then whispered, "I have a hook-up with this guy in Vancouver. He wants me to invest with him, and the return on the investment is really quick. I saw him work with one other guy, and now the guy's ahead $10,000. I thought since we were cool I would split the investment and the profit with you."

It all sounded a little too good to be true, so I asked what we would be investing in. "Cocaine," Darrell confided under his breath, looking around to see who was standing nearby. Without delay, I shouted, "No!" and rattled off a list of don'ts to Darrell:

- Don't ask again … ever!
- Don't bring any of those people around me or my job!
- Don't carry any of that crap when you are around me!

With that said, I went back to the hustle and bustle of a busy television office and tried to put the entire idea out of my mind. Soon, I was back to my normal routine. I went to work, played ball when I could, and never gave another thought to "investing" in drugs.

It was our normal custom to play pick-up basketball every Saturday morning. One day, I stopped by Darrell's apartment to give him a lift to the old high school gym where we played. I buzzed the intercom, but the voice that rang me in didn't sound like Darrell. As I walked through the door, I saw something that would stay with me as long as I lived. There was Darrell, sitting at the kitchen counter. Directly in front of him was a small mountain of cocaine; next to it was a scale. Before this time, I had only seen that much cocaine in movies. Come to think of it, that was the only place I had ever seen the precise scale that dope dealers use for weighing drugs. As I started to sweat, my eyes darted around the room. Darrell looked like he had been up all night, the apartment needed cleaning, and lined up along the baseboard was what appeared to be thirty or forty ***stacks*** of money, more than I could count. My heart started to pound so hard I could hear it. I could see the police bursting through the door; arrest me along with Darrell, as if I had orchestrated the entire thing.

Before Darrell could open his mouth, I calmly started to speak. “Don’t call me, don’t come by my house or job, and if we are ever at the same place at the same time, I will leave.” I only saw Darrell once after that. The stress of drug dealing had aged him to the point where I almost didn’t recognize him.

I couldn’t help but recall Granddaddy’s story about life’s barbed wire. The day that I stood in the hot Arkansas dirt and thought out loud about inmates in that prison, I learned a valuable lesson. The barbed wire story made me understand that Darrell was truly at a “sticky” spot in his life. Had it not been for the vivid image of those prisoners being beaten in the dirt and Granddaddy’s story about how to avoid it, I might have fallen prey to the lure of easy money from selling drugs and gotten myself involved in his sticky place. Instead, I knew that I wanted no part of it.

Granddaddy trained me to look for a way to solve any “sticky” situation—a way that involves taking the high road, never the low road. It saved me that day, and it has saved me many times since. Granddaddy’s “Barbed Wire” philosophy has always helped me to get quickly past the sticky parts and back to the smooth parts of life.

General Cook "Granddaddy"

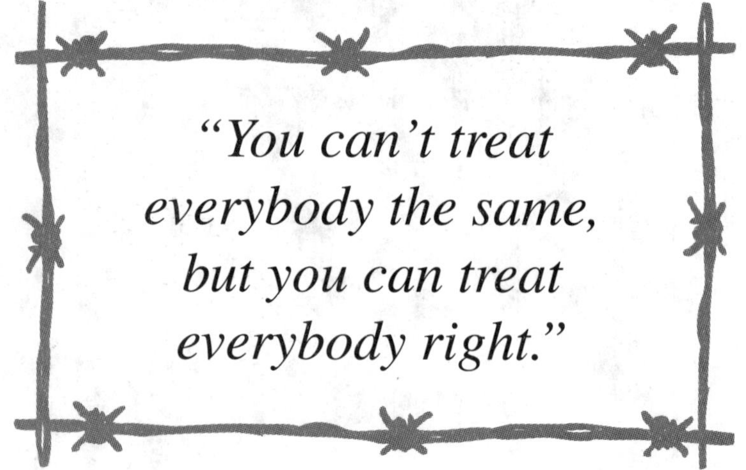

"You can't treat everybody the same, but you can treat everybody right."

Chapter 2

Treat 'em Right

When I was around eight or nine, granddaddy owned one of the prettiest horses I have ever seen. It seemed to me that he was at least as tall as the house. He was black—so black that his coat had a blue sheen, with a white star in the middle of his forehead and one white stocking.

I thought that a horse this handsome deserved a name to match, like Black Beauty, or Champion, or King. Surely every name that suggests majesty should have been considered for this outstanding animal, but Granddaddy called him Walter. Just plain Walter. It occurs to me now that the name he chose had something to do with the love-hate relationship between them. Granddaddy wasn't about to have a horse with a fancier name than his own. He wasn't about to have a horse that could get the best of him in a "difference of opinion," either.

You see, there were days when Walter made it plain that he didn't feel like being ridden. Each time granddaddy approached him with the saddle,

Walter tossed his head and stepped away. Granddaddy spoke sternly to him and tried again. Walter stepped away. This yes-you-will, no-I-won't dance could continue for what seemed like an hour. Eventually, granddaddy became exasperated and his arms grew tired from holding the heavy saddle. He paused to rest and regroup. Just as he turned to walk away, Walter nipped him on the back, right through his shirt, as if to say, "Well, we know who has the upper hand here, don't we!"

Granddaddy whirled around, slapped the horse smartly across the nose, and the two of them stared hard at each other. Walter got the message. Without a single wasted motion, granddaddy flung the saddle across Walter's back, tightened the cinch, put a foot in the stirrup, flung the other leg over Walter's back, and he was on board. The two of them rode away as if nothing had happened.

One day, granddaddy and I took a long ride into the countryside, an excursion that we had been planning for a long time. Granddaddy rode Walter, and I was mounted on an old, gray, sway-backed mare whose name I can't remember. Walter looked absolutely regal. He had an elegant, flowing mane and a long tail that he would raise just an inch or so when he was excited, as he was today. It almost seemed as if he were showing off for the old mare and I, who were following close behind. With every step the mare took, I bounced higher and higher, while Granddaddy and Walter looked like something you'd see in a movie—every movement perfection.

We rode for hours into areas of the country I had never seen before, and we talked about everything under the sun. I asked Granddaddy all the questions I could think of, and, as usual, he answered every one, never once complaining or making me think my questions were foolish or tiresome. Times like this were precious to me—times when there was nothing to do but talk and listen to each other, times when I had him all to myself. I didn't know it then, but I would remember them forever.

Before long, a truck came speeding down the road toward us from the opposite direction. The dusty road and ramshackle truck made dirt fly up everywhere. As the truck drew closer, it slowed down, moving past us very slowly. Then, it stopped and backed up. The driver was a white man, not one of those I had seen in town. He gave us a look different from any that I'd seen before, too, and he even gave off a different feeling. I didn't like him, but I didn't know why.

When he was directly opposite us, the driver leaned out of the window and said, "That's a mighty fine hoss you got there, boy. Who that hoss belong to?"

My granddaddy signaled Walter to stop and said nothing for a second or two. He seemed to slump a little in the saddle. Then, in a voice I had not heard before, he slowly and methodically said, "Much obliged, boss. This here hoss belong to boss Freeman over yonder in Varner county."

"Well, you tell him he got hisself one of the finest pieces of hoss flesh I ever seen, hear?"

Granddaddy forced a tight smile, touched his hat, chucked the reins, and Walter took off at a trot. I sat there for a second, utterly dumbfounded, before giving the mare a little kick with my heels to catch up with Granddaddy. I had another question, more urgent than any I had asked earlier.

"Granddaddy, Granddaddy, wait! Why didn't you tell that man Walter was *your* horse?"

He stopped, sitting tall in the saddle again, and looked me straight in the eye. "By hammers, son," he said. "There's something I learned a long time ago. You can't treat everybody the same, but you can treat everybody right. The way I treated that man was right for him. You see, he can only appreciate Walter if he thinks I don't own him. But I don't have to tell people Walter is mine in order to appreciate him. Gregory, it saddens me to say it, but some people in this world are not going to be happy about your success. So don't ever be a show-off about anything you have been fortunate enough to get. And don't go around trying to change people, either. Take them as they come, and you'll avoid a lot of trouble."

Years later, when I started with Xerox, I dreamed about and wrote goals to someday own a Mercedes convertible sports car. In Memphis, you didn't see that many Mercedes, and you certainly didn't see very many Mercedes sports cars. To own a car of this magnitude would certainly be the equivalent of owning a horse like Walter. I could be my Granddaddy in Memphis…owner of the most impressive transportation in town!

To get there, though, I first had to own and maintain two older Mercedes and work my way up. The first was a tan, 1968, 280 sedan, purchased from an older gentleman in Jonesboro, Arkansas, not far from Memphis. Having found the car in the want ads late on Sunday, I had to drive from Memphis to Jonesboro that night. I felt that if I didn't go immediately. Someone would surely snatch it first. Fifteen hundred dollars later, I owned my first Mercedes.

A year later, I sold it for a tidy profit and jumped into my next Mercedes. This one, sold to me by my mechanic, was a 1973 blue, 280 sedan. I felt that I had arrived! It was a beautiful royal blue with a navy blue leather interior that you could smell as soon as you opened the door. With all its beauty, this car was still short of my goal. After six months, I put the "blue beauty" on the market and purchased a silver blue, Mercedes SL…my dream car.

It was a warm, sunny Memphis morning when I drove it into the Xerox parking lot. I glided out of my new car and walked backwards toward the building, never taking my eyes off my new and most treasured possession. I had only been in the office for two minutes when Sklar Brower approached me. Sklar worked in a new division within Xerox, and we had become friendly. His first words were, "Hey, I saw you driving in this morning, and your smile had more shine than that new car!"

In a flash, I was back on the dirt roads of my Granddaddy's farm. I saw him on that horse and I saw again the penetrating stare of the truck driver. As I drifted back I realized that it wasn't Sklar's comment that bothered me. He had been more than a friend to me. What bothered me was the way that some of the senior sales people had treated me when Xerox hired me. I refused to look at their ill treatment of me as racial, I knew many people who happened to be Southern and they weren't racist in the least. Besides I reasoned, it wasn't just me, I saw it happen to women. They were also excluded from the "club" or the "good ole boy network." I looked at my fellow Xerox teammates as being competitive. Never offering help, very seldom-giving help when I asked for it and in general keeping a distance reserved for people you don't like or don't want to be friends with. It was one of those things I filed in the back of my mind. Today's conversation made me remember what happened to Granddaddy on that hot dusty road. It probably wasn't Sklar I needed to worry about; my thoughts of protection should have been reserved for the few negative types I encountered when my Xerox career started.

Not knowing how to handle the moment I immediately told Sklar that the car belonged to a friend, and I was just driving it for the day. The next day, I drove a used Chevy I had owned for years. I knew that my granddaddy was right. No matter how politely people smiled, the competitive nature of "some" Xerox sales people would not allow them to accept that car as mine. They would resent it and me for having it. I had forgotten granddaddy's words for a while, but now I remembered: You can't change some people…you have to treat them in a way they can accept.

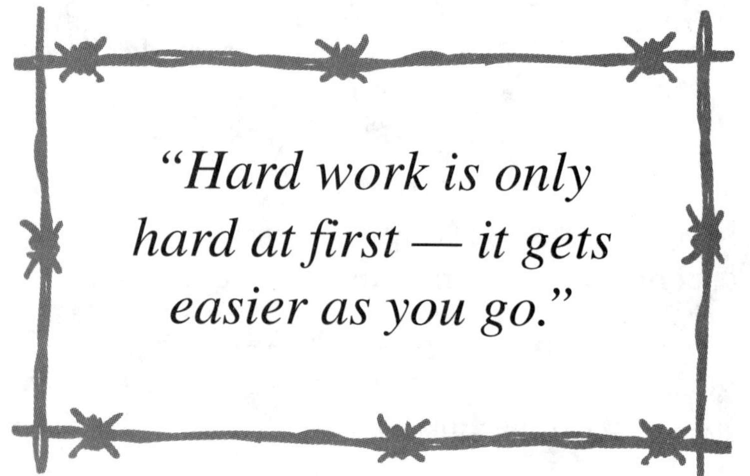

"Hard work is only hard at first — it gets easier as you go."

Chapter 3

Hard Work Gets Easier

I have never seen anyone work as hard as Granddaddy. Up at the crack of dawn, he would say his morning prayers, then get into his working clothes: khaki pants, long-sleeved khaki shirt, lace-up brogan work boots, a straw hat, and a handkerchief tucked neatly into his back pocket. After a quick breakfast, he was ready to tackle the day's work.

Some days, that work was cutting sugar cane, and no one could do it like Granddaddy. Because cane stalks grow densely to a height of about six feet, little or no air circulates inside the rows. Once you enter the field, you cut and sweat until you come out the other end of the row; one row of cutting seemed like it took half a day. But Granddaddy hit those rows of sugar cane like a human dynamo, slinging that blade and moving down the line with amazing accuracy. Sometimes he would sing while he cut, other times he would whistle, but always he was way ahead of the rest of us.

When he got to the end of the row, he waited for us to catch up. One by one, we emerged from the field to see him standing there, soaked in sweat. Pulling the handkerchief from his back pocket, he would take off his hat and wipe his brow. “Mmm-hmm. Just feel that breeze. That’s better than air conditioning!” We must have looked a bit doubtful, because he smiled. “You know, boys, the thing about hard work is, there’s nothing hard about it, but the beginning. Once you get started, it gets easier as you go. Let’s get back in there so we can get to the easy part.”

The words are deeply etched in my memory. Every time I’m faced with what seems to be a difficult task, I repeat them: “It looks like hard work right now, but it’s only hard at first. The more I do it, the easier it will be.”

On another day, we were plowing cotton using Granddaddy’s beloved John Deere tractor. Naturally, he drove and I sat next to him. Suddenly, he stopped the tractor, leaped off, and started to run and jump all over the place. For what seemed like an eternity, he ran, hurdled cotton stalks and then dived into the hot Arkansas dirt. Now I was really scared. Was he having some kind of fit? Should I try to help him somehow?

Then, Granddaddy stood up, covered in dust and dirt, but laughing out loud. In his right hand he held something, and as he came closer I could see that he was holding it by its long ears. When he handed me my new pet—a small, brown, rather terrified rabbit, I was thrilled. As he dusted himself off, he said, "You know, it took some work to catch this fellow…but only for a little while." Then he smiled. "It does get easier."

When the Xerox Corporation hired me, I was hoping it would get easier. I had gotten off to a rocky start, because I was so nervous that I failed the entrance examination. Ron Fisher, the branch sales training manager, pulled me to the side and gave me the bad news. Apparently I wasn't the first to fail, so Ron suggested that I relax and come back the next day to take the test over. I did, and I passed.

But it didn't stop there. After three months of in-branch training, I was sent to Leesburg, Virginia, where the famous Xerox University was located. A leader in sales training, Xerox had created a national school for its employees. It was like nothing I had ever seen. As you drove onto the grounds, it looked like a space ship. It was an octagonal building, positioned below the rest of landscape, and the lighting made it look like something from Star Trek, about to blast off.

Once inside, you were given a room, told what time meals were served, and then began three weeks of intense sales training. As if things weren't bad enough, I failed the first day's sales demonstration. The goal was to do a role-play while demonstrating one of the copiers in the Xerox line of "features-rich" products. After a series of chortles, grunts and snorts, I finally just froze, completely unable to remember any of the script I had practiced 1,000 times before. I felt both stupid and embarrassed.

Rather than enjoying a big dinner and lots of laughs with my new friend, James Brown, I decided to go to my room and remain there until I figured out how to get on track. James had just graduated from Harvard and seemed to have things together. Either that or he just didn't care. One thing I knew for sure, I could not hang out with James and act like nothing was wrong. I had to figure this out, and I had to do it fast.

A feeling came over me that I had only heard my Granddaddy talk about. I was in the unenviable position of wishing for a thing and not being ready to receive it. Pacing back and forth in my basketball shorts, my feet easily covered a mile of the industrial grade carpet Xerox had put in our rooms. I finally decided that no undetectable negative wind was blowing over my life. What I needed to do was the same thing I would need to do if I wanted to be a success at Xerox. I simply needed to work harder.

That night, I didn't get to bed until well past three a.m. I presented that speech and reviewed that demonstration until I was falling asleep standing up. In the back of my mind, I could hear Granddaddy's voice: "Hard work can't see failure. Hard work won't even recognize it." When I walked into the classroom the next day, I was ready. I delivered a demonstration so good I wanted to buy from myself!

That taste of success lasted as long as I was behind the protective walls of Xerox University. When I got back to the sweltering heat of Memphis in the summer, I faced a new challenge. I was assigned to a senior sales representative, Lewis Weiss. Lewis was great to work with, but his territory had a few patches that weren't so great. My job was to ride with Lewis for a few days, then start to make cold calls on my own.

To prepare for this task, I decided I would look for a mentor—someone I could pattern myself after, someone who already held the position in Xerox that I wanted. It didn't take long before I fixed my sights on Tom Carr. Tom was a legend around the company. Not only did he lead the branch in sales, but he dressed the part, walked the walk, and talked the talk.

Tom Carr was everything I wanted to be at Xerox. After building up enough nerve, I approached him and introduced myself. "Could I have some time to talk to you about the business?" Without thinking twice, he looked at me and said, "Sure, kid. Meet me in the coffee shop Monday morning. 7:00 a.m. be okay?" "Sure," I said, knowing that 7:00 a.m. was the time I would normally just be getting up.

At a few minutes before 7 Monday morning, I was there. I sat in the empty coffee shop, looking around as if I were waiting for my high-school principal. Precisely at 7:00, Tom whirled in as if he was going to some important board meeting. Without even ordering coffee first, he looked hard at me and said, "So, you want to know what it takes to be successful at Xerox?" "Yeah," I replied softly, as if this were some kind of trick question. "Here's the secret, kid. Don't watch *Sixty Minutes!*" He stood up, turned on his heel, and started for the door.

"Wait!" I called after him. He moved back toward the table, smiling as he sat down. "Okay. I'm going to take it slow with you. Every Sunday, all across the mid-south area, at 6:55 p.m., the sales reps from Xerox tune in to see what's going to be on *Sixty Minutes.* At the same time, in my home office, I'm planning my work one to two weeks ahead. When Monday rolls around, they come into the office, stand around the coffee pot, and shoot the breeze about what was on *Sixty Minutes.* But I come in long before they do, hand in my paperwork and schedule to my manager, and head for my territory. So, if you want to be successful, kid, don't watch *Sixty Minutes!"*

I got the message. As soon as I left the coffee shop, I began to change my habits. Work had to come first. Planning had to come first. But I still needed a mentor, a role model. That's where Lewis came in. As I rode the territory with him, I began to observe and imitate everything he did. Lewis had one strength that stood out above all others; he was peerless at developing rapport, and he did it at all levels. Absolutely no one was omitted. If they were in an office he called on, they got his attention.

Keep in mind that we were working in the South, where some people (certainly not all, but many) have been conditioned to react unfavorably to those who are racially or ethnically different from themselves. Lewis was Jewish, and not everyone accepted that. I am Black, and not everyone accepted that. But what I saw in Lewis was the same thing I saw in Granddaddy, who felt that if a person was prejudiced, it was just because they hadn't met him yet. He approached everyone as if they were going to love him…and so did Lewis.

So, by this time, I was well armed. I had picked up a valuable lesson from Tom Carr, and I had been assigned to a man who reinforced a lesson that would benefit me enormously. My ability to win people over, even those who had been taught that they shouldn't like me, helped make me a success in a city where most people in my situation would have failed. I maintained my self-discipline about getting to the office and to the territory early. Within my first few months on the job, I sold one of Xerox's largest copiers, and no one was more excited about my success than Lewis.

Lewis remains one of my dearest friends. He is to me what Mr. Freeman was to my Granddaddy. Because of Lewis, because of Tom, and because of my own willingness to learn and persist, the hard work at Xerox got easier.

Later that year, I told James Brown about my recent struggles, and he laughed so hard I had to shake him. His attitude about Xerox was different from everyone else's. He told me that what he really wanted to do was work in broadcasting. He was willing to do whatever it took, work as hard as he needed to work, in order achieve it. When I later went to work for CBS in marketing, James joined NBC, doing small segments during NBA games. The last time I saw him, he was running around the Key Arena at a Seattle Supersonics game, breathing hard and sweating as he carried heavy equipment to the next shot.

Some of you may have seen James; as I write this, he is now part of the Fox Sports Network. On some Sundays, I watch James, Terry Bradshaw, and Howie Long clowning on the air. James is still the same fun-loving guy. However, his hard work has paid off. Because of his own persistent efforts, life has gotten easier for him, and he is able to do what he loves for a living.

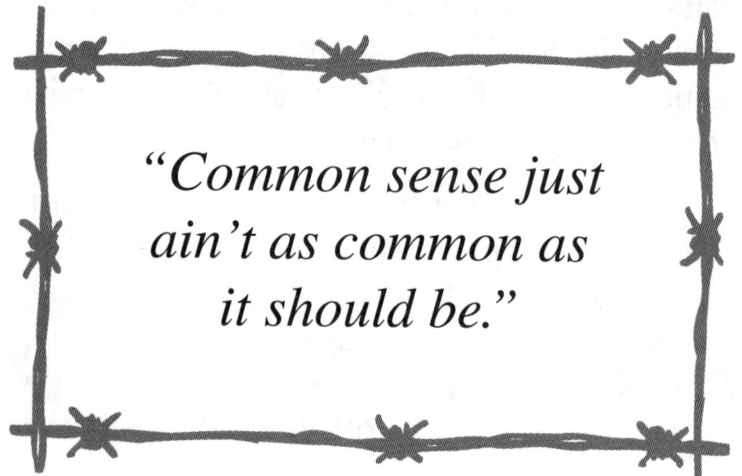
"Common sense just
ain't as common as
it should be."

CHAPTER 4

Everyday Genius

Almost everyone who knew my Granddaddy, General Cook, had good things to say about him. They talked about how much they liked him, what a great storyteller he was, the way he always tried to help others, and, above all, how intelligent he was. His intelligence, I heard over and over, towered over everything else. Yet, I don't think Granddaddy saw himself as unusually intelligent. What he believed he had plenty of and valued highly in others was common sense, which he said was "not nearly as common as it should be."

The stories I remember about Granddaddy begin around the time of the great depression. By then, he had been farming and doing business in Varner, Arkansas for some time. Granddaddy was not a worrier, but he gradually noticed that "trading" (his word for the buying and selling upon which his living depended) was becoming more and more difficult. Many things were growing scarce or expensive, and he was concerned about not being able to provide for his family. As a result, during the summer before the depression hit, he decided to build another smokehouse on his property.

In those days, smokehouses were used to cure and store meat for long periods. They were the no-power predecessors of today's meat lockers and freezers. Granddaddy raised and slaughtered several kinds of livestock in order to keep meat on the family's table and both smokehouses full.

As time passed and the shadow of the Depression grew darker, many local farmers fell on hard times—harder than most could remember. It was the first time they had ever seen bread lines, soup kitchens, and men begging for money or work. Fear of poverty spread like a virus across the entire country, and having enough to eat became many families' top priority. Soon, his smokehouses became so valuable that Granddaddy took to guarding them at night. Armed with a shotgun, he and his two eldest sons alternated standing watch to protect them. As increasing numbers of people began to barter valuables for food, many of them traded with Granddaddy. Soon, word spread around the county that General Cook had food to trade, but only in exchange for one thing.

Granddaddy would call it "just good common sense," but I call it everyday genius. Because he watched what was happening around him and could anticipate both short- and long-term needs, not only had he cured and stored enough meat to feed an Army, but he was smart enough to exchange it for something that would help him grow: land. With more land, he could breed his current stock of animals, increase their numbers, and trade on a larger scale.

Granddaddy also considered it good common sense to think for yourself. He lived in a part of the country where business was traditionally conducted informally, via conversation and a handshake, but when he traded, he insisted on written deeds of trust or contracts. This was considered unusual, but granddaddy didn't care. He was an unusual man. In the Deep South, few Black farmers owned any land at all. However, granddaddy came to own 120 acres of prime farmland. He didn't work for other people, and he wasn't a sharecropper. He was his own boss. His own man.

After he married and his 13 children came along, granddaddy would gather the family around him—sometimes seven girls, sometimes six boys, many times all of them together—to tell true stories about his life. Sometimes these anecdotes were funny, but most were intended to teach important lessons. Granddaddy believed that the lion's share of what you needed to know was learned at home, not at school. He said school gave you "a book learning," but parents gave you "a life learning."

Now and then, when the kids were clustered around him, he would joke about his own lack of education. He said, "If I had been lucky enough to get a book learning, I would be one of the richest men in the world. Either that, or I would have learned all about what I wasn't supposed to do!"

Granddaddy made no secret of the fact that his ability to think and use common sense set him apart. It was a legitimate source of pride, and he gave himself credit where it was due. I remember him as clearly as if it were yesterday, describing one of his competitors by saying, "Gregory, I can think twice to his once!" Granddaddy's mind was quicker than most, because he trained it to be.

He also trained himself to develop an amazing ability to recall facts. The mnemonic device he used was to tie all the important details to a story. Later, when he would repeat the story, the facts would come flying back. "Do what you know to do," he would say. "If you don't know, then ask. But remember the answer, and tie it to a story so you'll be sure."

The first profitable story I remember telling was the one that landed my first job. It was my first season playing organized basketball. I had gone out for the team and made it, but was told the school couldn't provide basketball shoes. That left me with a choice; I could quit or find a way to come up with new Converse All-stars, the popular shoe of the day. Converse All-stars were the "Nike" of that era, and carried a price tag of approximately fifteen dollars.

As I started my walk home from school that cool fall day, I thought about how I could get the money. My mother was not going to part with fifteen of her hard-earned dollars for something as frivolous as basketball shoes. I was so sure she didn't have the money, that I couldn't even ask. As I walked along kicking the fallen leaves, my thoughts turned to Granddaddy. I wondered what he would do. A man who made a living out of nothing would certainly be able to solve this small problem. I kicked some leaves and thought. I walked, kicked more leaves, and then I got an idea.

Across the train tracks was a neighborhood much more prosperous than mine. We called the residents of this neighborhood "the rich people." I decided to go over to the rich people and knock on doors. There was no answer at the first house. After unsuccessfully trying a few more houses, I finally heard steps from inside, and knew someone was coming. The steps got louder. Then the door swung open, and a voice shouted, "Yeah?" I stood rooted to the spot, feeling something between amazement and fears, as I looked at a heavy-set man in rumpled t-shirt and baggy underwear.

"I'll rake your le-le-leaves if you'll buy me some b-b-basketball shoes so I can play ball this year," I stammered.

"Not interested," the man in the doorway barked.

As he slammed the door, I just stood there, not quite understanding what had happened. I tried to figure out what to do. Suddenly, I clenched my teeth and knocked again. This time, I did it with more determination. I stopped when I could hear those heavy footsteps again, pounding as they came toward the door.

As he snatched the door open. I stepped into the doorway. He scowled at me. "I *said* I am not interested, kid!"

"But I really need these shoes. I can't play basketball without them. They're Converse All-stars,"

I said. There was a long, painful silence. It seemed to go on for hours, but was probably only seconds. I looked at this man standing there in his shorts. He looked back at me. We stood there staring at each other without blinking. Then, his eyes darted back toward the living room of the house.

"Honey, could you come here for a minute," he said over his shoulder.

Soon, I heard more footsteps. As a woman approached the doorway, the man said, "Tell her what you told me."

"If you buy me some shoes to…" I began.

"No, not that part," he said. "Tell her the part you said when I came back the second time."

I rummaged through my mind, trying to figure out what he was trying to get me to say, and then it came to me. "I said I really need these shoes, so I can play basketball. They're Converse All-stars."

The two of them looked at each other and smiled. "Well, son, I think I might be able to help get you a pair of Converse All-stars. You got a rake?"

"No," I said. "I live over in the projects, and we don't even have leaves!"

The two of them began to laugh. Mr. And Mrs. Straight (their real names) helped me get my first pair of All-stars, and I helped them keep their leaves raked up. What began as a hostile first impression was the start of a relationship that lasted through my high school years.

But the real story is that I felt like a genius. I had solved a problem and created my first job, in one fell swoop. Deep inside, I felt like my granddaddy. There I was, on the rich side on town, telling my own true story and making genius work for me.

Mr. & Mrs. General Cook

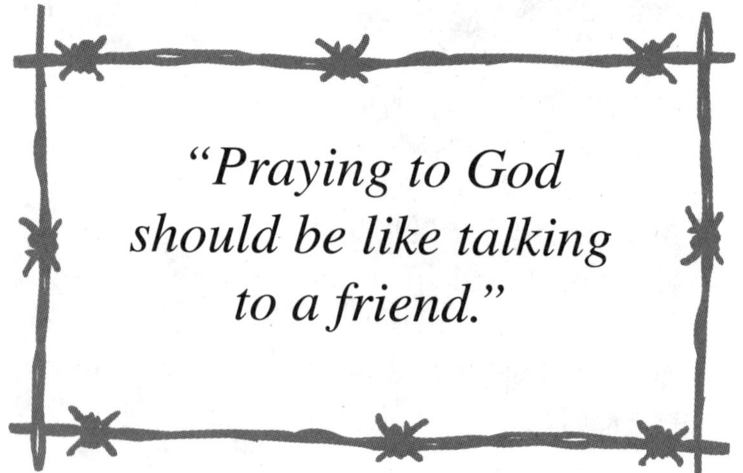
"Praying to God
should be like talking
to a friend."

Chapter 5

Getting Into Position

It was early morning, cool and still dark outside. At granddaddy's, the day always started very early. As I lay in bed getting used to being awake, I thought I could hear him saying his morning prayers. That was enough to get me moving, so I jumped out of my deep feather mattress and the soft, warm nest it made for me. When I tiptoed into his bedroom, I saw that he was in what I thought of as his praying position—on his knees at the side of the bed, elbows on the bed, forehead resting carefully on the base of his open palms.

I slipped into the position beside him. Not knowing the right words to say, I tried to repeat whatever he said. Some of the words I understood and could say correctly; others I wasn't sure of, so I just mumbled and hoped I came close. Mostly, what I wanted was to be in the praying position with him, so I stole a sideways glance at him, adjusted my position slightly, prayed a little, peeked again and prayed a little more.

With the tender smile of a father (I often pretended and felt that he was), he looked over at me and asked, "Son, do you know how to talk to God?" I quickly assured him I did, and demonstrated by squeezing my eyes shut and rattling off the "prayer speech" I had learned at an earlier age: "Our father, who *are* in heaven, *holly* be thy name…."

Granddaddy stood up and put his hand on my shoulder. "Son, you don't need to memorize anything. All you need to know is that praying to God and talking to God are exactly the same thing. I talk to Him many times during the day. Sometimes I ask for help for my family, my friends, and sometimes for myself. Then there are times when I just talk to God as my friend. Tell him what's on my mind. What's worrying me or what's making me feel good."

He paused for a second and motioned for us to start getting ready for the workday. "Gregory, there are many ways to look at prayer, but I see it as talking to an old friend, and that friend is God." As he started out of the room, he added, to me or to God, or, more likely, to both of us, "And you know, when you have God as a friend, you will never, never be alone."

The Cook Family minus two of the kids.

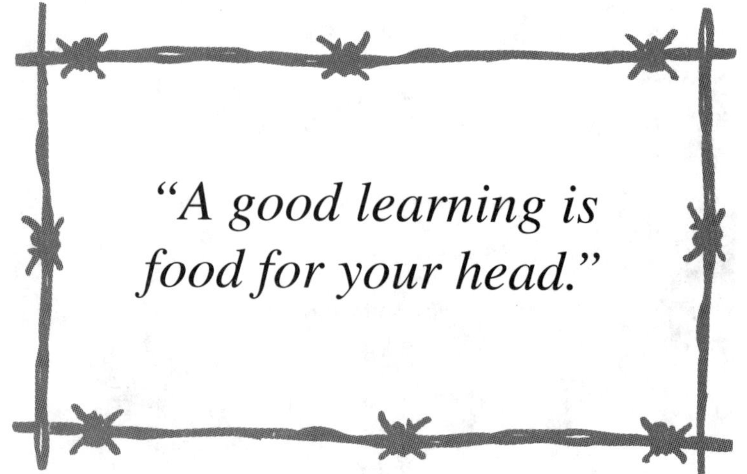
"A good learning is
food for your head."

Chapter 6

Soul Food

With two adults and thirteen children living there and a successful farm surrounding it, it seems inevitable that the Cook house would become a beehive of activity. Multiply thirteen children times one or two friends each, and you create an incredibly busy household. With all that energy centered in and around Granddaddy's house, children from nearby farms were drawn to it, too. Sometimes it felt like a small town all by itself.

My Aunt Juanita remembers playing at the house with some of her friends. They had been there most of the day, but their play stopped when it was time for dinner. Just after the family sat down to eat, Granddaddy pulled up in his truck. He hated to be late for meals.

As he walked up to the house, he noticed the group of kids sitting outside, watching and waiting while the Cook family ate. In the kitchen, he took Grandmamma aside and asked her to serve the children who were outside, too. The Depression was in full swing. He knew it was likely that there would be no dinner waiting for those children when they arrived home, which was why they were sitting around his house at mealtime instead of heading home.

Grandmamma quickly explained that she planned to feed the kids outside after the family had eaten. With thirteen at the table, there was no space for extra chairs. Granddaddy persisted. "No," he said. "They all have to eat at the same time. All together. Let some of them sit on the floor or in the kitchen. We don't want those who are fed last to think they are getting leftovers or handouts. We don't want them to feel uncomfortable or embarrassed." After dinner, all the kids would gather around him to listen to him tell stories or offer advice. He called it "food for your head."

Because he was such a marvelous storyteller, he often found himself in the center of an attentive circle wherever he went. When we went into town, Granddaddy would get his hair cut and tend to his business while I would roam freely, usually in search of something good to eat. As I went from store to store (eight in the whole town), I heard people say, "That's General's boy," causing what little chest I had to expand. Being his relative made me feel almost famous.

When I went back to the barbershop to meet him, there would always be a group sitting around Granddaddy. As each man spoke or asked a question, he would turn his eyes and one hundred percent of his attention to that person. He regarded each comment, each man, as valuable, and they loved and respected him for it. When he responded to something they had said, he would often reach out and touch them on the arm or shoulder as he made his point.

Granddaddy understood, instinctively, that people, no matter how young or old, needed to feed their minds as regularly as they fed their bodies. And he knew, just as surely, that how we treat each other and ourselves is the most important way we feed our souls.

I can still remember one special time when my head and soul were fed. My closest sister, Renita, had received a double dose of bad news. After ten years and three children, she was in the middle of a divorce. If that wasn't enough, she had been diagnosed with breast cancer.

When I heard the news, I insisted that she move herself and the kids from Little Rock to

Seattle. I changed my bachelor-pad home into something that resembled the Huxstable's residence on the old "Bill Cosby Show." We became real family, going to church, making dinner, singing and dancing together…we even got a dog. As we worked together to beat the cancer, we became even closer as a family.

The next step was harder. Renita had to be admitted to the hospital, undergo extensive testing, and, eventually, chemotherapy. Anyone who has had an experience with cancer in or close to their family knows how difficult this can be. Renita had undergone a tremendous physical change. It wasn't just the loss of her hair. Her face, her body, and her spirit all showed the ravaging effects of cancer.

At one point, her condition had deteriorated drastically, and she requested that I be the only one allowed to visit her. For days and nights that blurred together, I would go to work and then visit her. I became a fixture in the hospital. Doctors and nurses alike were subject to my daily interrogations and battery of questions. I worked the staff and prayed for Renita as if my life as well as hers depended on it.

After a year of bad times and grave doubt, there came a ray of sunshine. Renita's condition began to improve. One day, when she called me to the hospital, I could hear the lift in her voice. She told me that she had decided that her health had improved to the point where she could now accept visitors. "But, Greg," she added, "make sure that you get me some make-up and a wig. I don't want anyone to see me like this." For the first time in my life, I openly cried and smiled at the same time. I was saddened by the losses Renita had suffered, but overjoyed with life and the beauty of my baby sister.

My first stop was Nordstrom. I went straight to the cosmetic area, where the well-groomed women with the white, almost clinical looking, jackets presided. "Excuse me, I need to get some make-up," I said, as one woman turned to me with a curious stare. "Oh, it's not for me!" I explained. "It's for my sister. We look alike, and our color is about the same. I'm from a predominately black family." *A predominately black family*—where did *that* come from? I was more flustered than I realized.

Sensing my nervousness, the saleswoman began to ask me some questions about my sister. As we talked, I became more comfortable. Soon, she told me that she had dealt with cancer in her family, too. We shared stories, some good, some bad, and then I bought some makeup. I left feeling less alone in my struggle.

That evening, I arrived at the hospital in a rush. I wanted to make sure Renita was happy with everything I had purchased. I was still uncertain about my ability to buy makeup and get it right. As I neared her room, I heard voices. Panic set in. My first thought was that some complication had occurred. My heart was pounding as I pushed the door open. But there, applying makeup to my sister's face, was the same clerk who had helped me at Nordstrom! She explained that our conversation had moved her, to the point where she wanted to help. She had my name from the sales slip, and remembered the hospital I had mentioned. From there, it was a simple matter to track Renita down. Talk about going the extra mile!

It was amazing. We had exchanged *food for the head* that day, and we were both nourished by it. Because our spirits were lifted, now, Renita was being nourished by it, too.

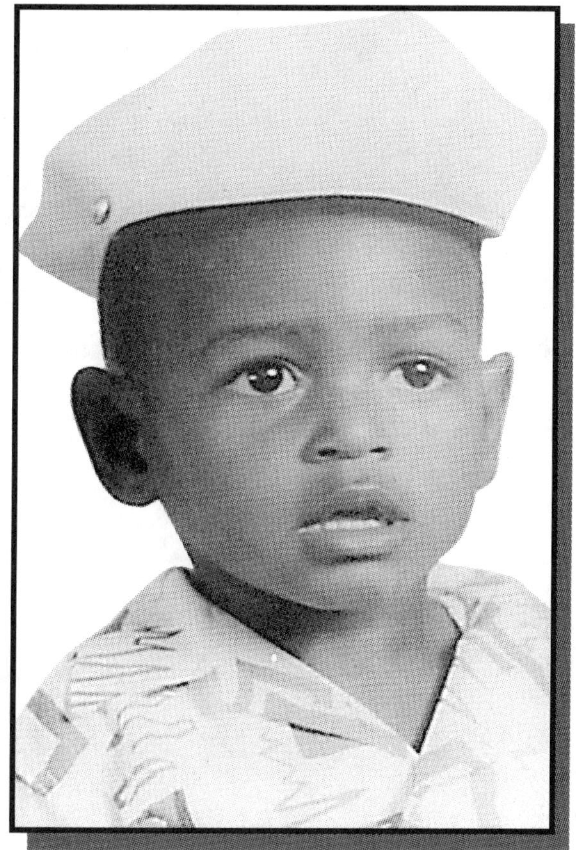

Me around the time I met and lived with Granddaddy

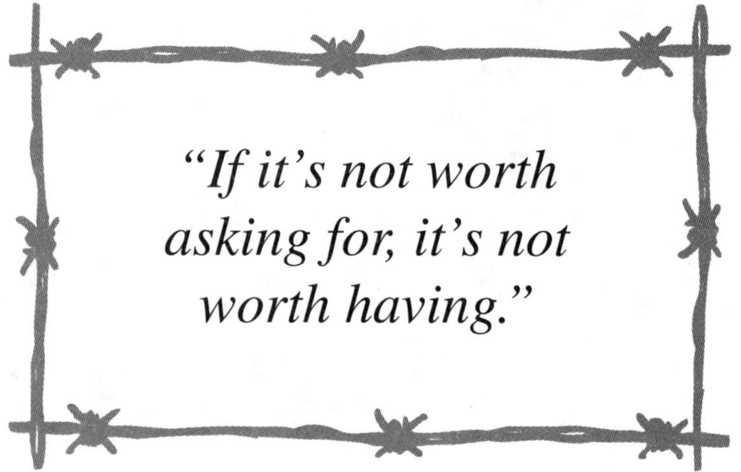
*"If it's not worth
asking for, it's not
worth having."*

Chapter 7

What You Have Depends on How You Get It

One summer, our cousin from Berkley, California joined my brother, Glen, and me at Granddaddy's. We called him Junior, after Granddaddy's second son, Alvin. Junior was two years older than I was, and he had a trendy, California-hipness about him. Even though he was a newcomer to the farm, Glen and I followed his lead in all our daily activities: exploring, swimming, running, riding, camping, and stealing.

That's right, stealing, but just once. Granddaddy's good friend and neighbor, Mr. Freeman, had a flourishing, easily accessible watermelon patch. When the melons were ripe, the adventure of stealing some and getting away with it was too alluring to resist. As we had imagined, it was a cinch. We crept into the patch, each of us broke off a good-sized melon from the vine, and we hightailed it out of there.

As we ran, we discussed a strategy. The loft of Granddaddy's barn would be the perfect place to hold our feast without being discovered, but first, we needed silverware and saltshakers. Of course, we missed the irony: a daring gang of rough-and-ready watermelon thieves, too refined to eat without proper seasoning and utensils!

We decided that Glen would take the melons to the loft, while Junior and I would head for the house. I would find some reason to distract grandmamma, while Junior stuffed the utensils and salt into his pockets. Again, we pulled it off without a hitch. Within minutes, we were sitting on bales of hay, eating watermelon until we were so stuffed we could hardly walk. There was, however, one small problem we hadn't anticipated: It was almost time for supper. Now, supper at granddaddy's was much different than dinner. Supper was the big, formal meal of the day, at which we discussed anything of importance.

As with every meal, we didn't immediately sit down. We came to the table, stood behind our chairs, bowed our heads, and listened respectfully as granddaddy asked the Lord to bless the food.

Then, we went around the table and each of us had to quote a verse or part of a verse from the Bible (the one I usually chose, because it was short and easy to remember, was "Jesus wept.") Only then could supper officially begin.

Of course, I could hardly eat a bite, and Glen merely nibbled. Amazingly, Junior wolfed his meal as if he was going to be executed the next day. No one seemed to notice that Glen and I were only playing with our food. As the minutes passed, I grew drowsy and drifted off into the sounds of clinking silverware and conversation. Maybe a nap after supper would be just the thing. Suddenly, Granddaddy's voice entered my consciousness like a bolt lightning, as he casually mentioned that he had just come from Mr. Freeman's place.

The eyes of the infamous watermelon gang darted up from our plates, and as we glanced at each other, I have no doubt that we were all seeing the same thing: stark terror. Before anyone could say another word, I blurted out, "We're *sorry,* Granddaddy! I don't know why we did it! I don't know why I did it! I'm really, really sorry…."

Granddaddy raised his hand, palm out, and I knew I needed to stop talking. "Never—and I mean *never*—take anything that doesn't belong to you! *If it's not worth asking for, it's not worth having.* You have shamed my name, and all for the sake of taking something that we already have. If you wanted watermelons, we have a patch full of them." His voice rose, and then lowered again. "Do you hear me? *If it's not worth asking for, it's not worth having.*"

We sat motionless, heads hanging, flooded with shame and regret. "You know, years ago," Granddaddy went on, "I was guilty of stealing." Now he *really* had our attention. Granddaddy had actually done something wrong, and he was admitting it! "When I started to farm, I had to borrow money. The man who loaned it to me was Ned Harden. Harden looked over my land. We talked about how much it could produce, how much money I needed, and how I would pay him back after the harvest. This was just before the great depression, and after I paid Harden, there wouldn't be enough left to support my family. I figured out a way I could over-plant the land, fertilize it heavily, and make more from it than Harden and I had agreed on. Since Harden was a big man in the next town, I sold the overage someplace else so he wouldn't hear of it. The extra money helped support my family, but, in a sense, I stole from myself. I wasn't straight with Harden, and to this day I don't feel good about what I did."

That's Granddaddy, in a nutshell. How firm and fair he was in teaching us what we needed to know, including the simple wisdom of asking for what you want. How amazingly creative and resourceful he was, especially when it came to earning money. How he could take almost any situation and turn it into something more productive. How strong and clear his ethics were. I still don't think that what he did qualifies as stealing. Harden got paid, on time and in full. But, to Granddaddy, what you *didn't* say could be a lie, just as much as what you did. And just as bad as stealing something that didn't belong to you was robbing yourself of your own integrity.

When we returned to the city from our summer in the country, I was excited about getting back to school, because it meant that sports would begin again. One of my favorite activities was getting in shape for the season. During those times in particular, my brother, Glen, and I were close. We would walk to school, work out, discuss strategies and walk home, always together.

While we were walking home one evening, a police car pulled up beside us. In a matter of seconds, we were questioned, told to get in the car, and taken to police headquarters. When we arrived, we were immediately put in separate rooms for more questioning. Even though the questions were being asked in rapid-fire succession, I was able to surmise that a car had been stolen. As the police intensified their questions, I became more and more nervous. After going back and forth for what seemed like days, the police left me in the room by myself.

Sitting there, alone and scared, I thought about how unfair this was. I wondered why this was happening to Glen and me. Just then, the door swung open and one of the police officers quickly walked in and plopped a yellow legal pad on the desk. "Your brother has confessed to everything. See, he signed this statement." My eyes searched the page and there at the bottom was Glen's signature! I didn't know what it said above his name, and I didn't care. "Get my mother on the phone or I won't say another word," I shouted. "I can't speak for Glen, but I can speak for me, and I didn't steal anything, and I'm not going to say another word. You can do whatever you want, but I'm not going to talk anymore!"

He left the room, and within the hour my mother walked in, and was she angry! She shouted and shook her finger at the cops. She demanded to see their boss. Then, she took me by the arm, and we walked through the station looking for Glen. I remember one of the officers following behind us like a lost pup, but the rest of it was a blur. Soon we were headed home. All Mom could talk about was the audacity of the police, making Glen sign that statement that he didn't even understand!

Days later, the incident continued to bother me. I remembered how quickly I had admitted everything and apologized when I stole the watermelons. This time, even though I hadn't done anything wrong, I had an equal amount of resolve. Those watermelons helped me realize that I never wanted to let my family down again. Being wrong taught me how to stand tall and be strong when I was on the right side of right.

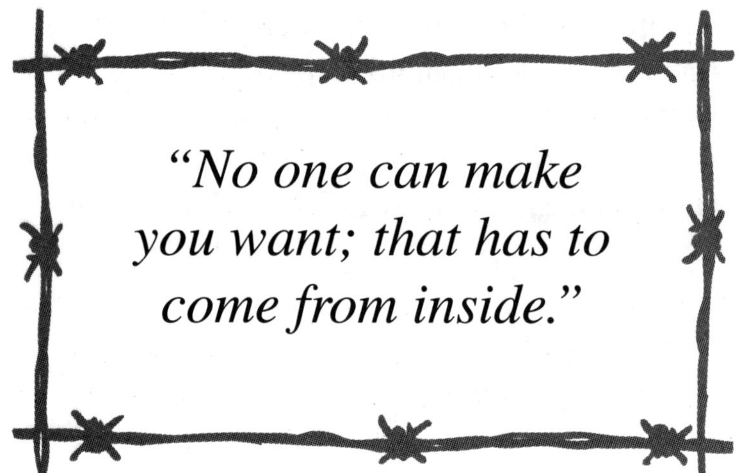
"No one can make
you want; that has to
come from inside."

Chapter 8

First You See It, Then You Can Be It

In the Bible and in Arkansas, everything has a season. There are times to plant and times to harvest. Cotton has its season, just as watermelons have theirs. As a rule, granddaddy rotated his crops for maximum yield. In addition to benefiting the soil, it enabled him to give something back to his community. Every season, he would plant an acre of land with a crop he would give away. If anyone else wanted to participate, they would receive an equal share of that season's corn, watermelons, sugarcane, etc.

Granddaddy was as much a teacher as a farmer, so he just naturally used his philosophy of sharing to teach kids the advantages of farming. Take the Hollomans, for example—a family that lived and worked on Granddaddy's property. They were given a house and a portion of the harvest in exchange for the work they did on the farm.

The commonly used term for this is "sharecropping," but granddaddy treated the entire Holloman family as if they were part of his own.

One day, he took the three eldest Holloman boys aside and gave them each an acre to farm. He told them that whatever they produced on that land was theirs, no strings attached. As sharecroppers, it was difficult if not impossible to do more than break even, granddaddy was giving them an opportunity to do more than just survive. He was giving them an opportunity to make a profit, and to use that profit to improve their lives.

As it turned out, only one of the Holloman boys took the offer to heart. While I was visiting early that spring, the two of us tilled, plowed, and planted a crop of watermelons. Later that summer, we took a bountiful harvest to sell in nearby towns. Gene and I made more money than we had ever imagined, but the other Holloman boy didn't have much to say.

Later, when we talked about that summer's turn of events, granddaddy said it was too bad that both of those boys couldn't see opportunity when it was standing right in front of them, but if they didn't want to see it, no one could make them. He would use the word *desire* over and over again. Desire, he believed, was what gave life to our actions, but desire had to be born from within.

"You can't make a person be something, if they can't see it. You can't make a person have something, if they don't want it. Each of us has to be able to see where we want to go in life. A few folks are lucky enough to be *born knowing*, but most of us see in someone else the thing that seems right for us. If you're one of those who are born without that vision, then you have to learn to imagine your life from the things around you. But nobody can make you see, nobody can make you want…that has to come from inside yourself."

I never knew how true that statement was until I came face to face with my own personal desire. Although it seemed small to everyone around me, basketball had become very big in my life. Because of a remarkable high school coach by the name of Oliver Elders, I had started to work out every day during my free period. Coach Elders taught me the basics of the game, changing the way I shot the ball, showing me how to catch it on my fingertips, demonstrating proper defense, and explaining how life was like a sport.

The workouts were good, but I felt I was doing it more for Coach Elders than for myself. I was there every day, running, jumping and sweating—but it felt mechanical. My heart wasn't really in it. Then, one day, I saw a basketball player who did things on the court I had never seen before. His name was Almer Lee. It was generally agreed that Almer was the best basketball player in the history of Arkansas basketball. Almer could:

- Dribble the ball as if were attached to his body,
- Shoot with either hand from 30 feet,
- Bounce the ball off his knees, chest, and then dunk it with both hands,
- Break most opponents' press defense by himself,
- Cause traffic jams as fans tried see him in the state tournament,
- Start a migration of Black athletes to the University of Arkansas that resulted in the great teams of the late 70s and 80s.

Stories are plentiful about Almer, but the one I want to tell concerns his effect on me. Almer was the first person to help me create a powerful desire. After we became friends by playing in summer league, Almer began to give me advice on how to improve. My first question was how he got to be so good. "I watched the guys at AM&N, (a neighboring Black college), and practiced every day until I could do everything I saw them do," he said. There was one guy in particular whom Almer would copy. His name was Red Allen, and he was a magician with the basketball.

Almer was only one year ahead of me in school, which, combined with his amazing ability, made it easy for me to listen to him and to follow his every move. From the day that he confided his secrets to me, I began to practice everything that Almer did. It didn't seem strange to me at the time, but Almer said that I was the only person who had ever asked him how to improve their game! I think he enjoyed being a mentor.

Soon, the lessons and self-discipline began to pay off. One day, while playing in an old, hot and almost deserted YMCA, Almer and I were placed on the same team. One of Almer's favorite plays was the "pick and roll," a play that allows one player to block the defensive player and "roll" to the basket for a pass. The play that stands out in my mind, one that typifies Almer, was a pick and roll where he completed a perfect pass to me. The result was twofold, I caught the pass, and finished with a mid-air, two-hand dunk, whereupon Almer shouted and ran out of the gym!

What made the play a source of motivation for Almer was that the person guarding me was Martin Terry. Martin was being heavily recruited by the University of Arkansas, and went on to set many scoring records that still stand. Almer used my dunk to motivate me and deflate the efforts of Martin's team. That was Almer, first a teacher and then a motivator.

I have used both lessons again and again. The first lesson—see what you want as clearly as possible to strengthen your personal desire; and the second—find someone who is already successful doing what you want to do and make them your mentor. These lessons enabled me to come out of nowhere to start as a freshman for Arkansas. I began the season knowing what I wanted. By using skills and attitudes learned from Almer, I was able to play at a level that even surprised me.

The lessons I learned are still with me today. When I want to achieve something, I always look first to make sure my goal is clear. By understanding both where I am and where I want to be, and developing a clear sense of my direction, I am self-motivated. Next, I find someone who is successful in the same endeavor from whom I can learn. I can take the fast track to success because I don't have to reinvent what already exists.

There are fine teachers all around us, but it all starts with desire. Here's how granddaddy told me I could increase desire:

- **"Write it on a paper bag."** Without the luxury of stationary, he often wrote things down on the brown paper bags that his supplies came in. He had stacks of these bags, and every day he would write on them about some new idea or venture.
- **"Read it after you pray."** Every morning and every night, Granddaddy said his prayers. On his knees, he would pray openly, as if God were right there in the room. Just before he went to sleep, he would reread the notes he had scribbled on those old brown paper bags.
- **"By the second Sunday."** To make sure he stayed on track, he gave himself deadlines to race against. In his mind, all time was measured beginning with Sunday. He would say, "I'll have it done by the first Sunday (second Sunday, etc.).
- **"Give some away."** Granddaddy believed that he could only receive

what he wanted when others got something of value in return. Knowing that others would benefit from his successes made him more confident and motivated.

- **"Look for the good stuff."** Every day, Granddaddy would look for the good things that happened in his life. He called it "Good Stuff," and the premise was that you couldn't be pulled down by negative thoughts if your mind was focused on the positive elements. He would say over and over, "Your head can't hold good and bad at the same time...so pick the good stuff."

The ideas were simple. As I look back, I can't remember a single time when my Granddaddy was sad or despondent. In fact, unless there was some problem that could affect his family, I never saw him get very upset. I was too young to realize it at the time, but his positive outlook and even disposition came from his belief in and use of these basic principles. I am eternally grateful to him for passing them along to me.

Cecil Winters "Aunt Cecil"

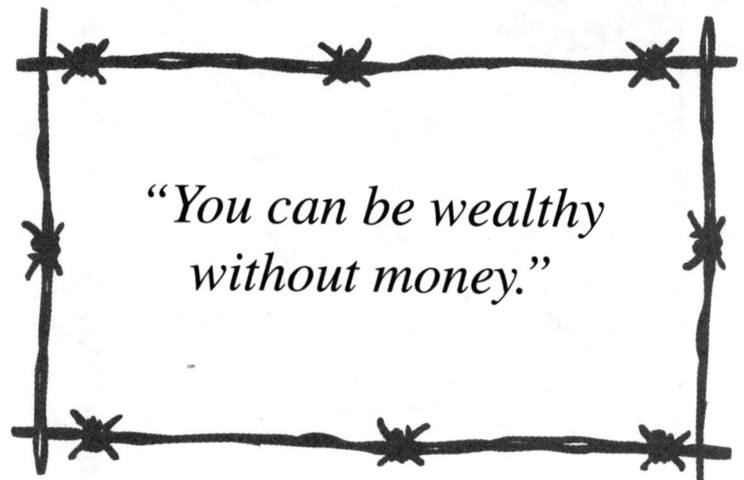
"You can be wealthy without money."

Chapter 9

The Theory of One

For as long as I can remember, granddaddy operated by the "Theory of One." It was a philosophy designed to facilitate a simple yet solid life: Worship one God, marry only once, buy only one house, one watch, one truck, and so on.

This theory affected the way he thought about almost everything, especially finances. Over and over again, he would say, "It is better to have the certain absence of future payments than the uncertain future of projected income. Buy it once!"

His reasoning was simple. Save your money to buy what you want. Don't buy on some "same as cash" credit plan, then spend your days worrying about what will happen if you have to miss a payment or trying to predict your financial future. When you do buy, buy something that is built to last, and take proper care of it so that it will. To make sure that he was always in a position to buy whatever he needed when he needed it, he became very good at earning and saving money.

At that time, Southern mill operators had established policies allowing them to pay black farmers less for crops than their white counterparts. Now, granddaddy had many associates—farmers and businessmen who liked and respected him enough to come to him for advice. After God, however, he only had one true friend with whom he shared everything, and that friend happened to be white. His name was Mr. Freeman.

Granddaddy and Mr. Freeman talked every day. Sometimes they went hunting together, sometimes they worked together, but whatever the reason, they had some kind of daily contact. Between them, they worked out a plan to get around the unfair mill payment policies.

At harvest time, most farmers hired temporary helpers to bring in the crops. These harvest hands were almost always black. Because of the distrust blacks held for most of the area's white people, Mr. Freeman had problems putting together a solid crew of workers, so Granddaddy used his influence to hire workers who would bring in Mr. Freeman's crops. Once harvested, Mr. Freeman and Granddaddy sat side by side and hauled both of their crops to the gin or mill. Mr. Freeman collected the higher white man's price for the entire load and passed Granddaddy's share along to him as soon as they were out of sight.

The Theory of One taught me a lot about money. It taught me even more about the value of a single, strong friendship. As a result, I have a rock-solid, thirty-year relationship with Willie Gregory. Willie and I have shared basketball, money, cars, women troubles, family joys, fashion trends, career ambitions, even serious health concerns. Through it all, we have enjoyed and supported each other, and there is no question that we always will.

In these days of conspicuous consumerism, heavy personal debt, and "disposable" relationships, Granddaddy's ideas about friendship and material possessions may seem old-fashioned. I remember questioning his Theory of One at the time, asking why he didn't want to own more and fancier things. But even today, I can't argue with his response: "By hammers, son! I am a wealthy man without all that. I have my family. I have a true friend. I have self-respect and respect from my community. And I'm wealthy because I own outright everything I will ever need."

*"Don't just do.
Be."*

CHAPTER 10

Change Your Mind, Change Your Life

So much of what Granddaddy said is still with me, yet I can recall so little of my formal college education. I guess that's because the education I received from Granddaddy was different—certainly more fun, and generally much more relevant. One of the most useful things he taught me was how to learn and teach through the use of stories, but the most valuable lesson of all has to be his concept of "being."

He would say, "Don't just do, son. *Be.* Everyone in the world will tell you what he or she thinks you should know, and what he or she thinks you should do. But the best education comes when you work on who you need to *be.* When you come to grips with your own being, everything else gets easier" :

- The man who asked whose horse Granddaddy was riding (because he thought it couldn't possibly belong to a black man) didn't bother Granddaddy. He knew, without a shadow of doubt, who and what he was.

- Being offered unfair prices for his crops didn't bother Granddaddy. He figured out a way around it without making trouble for anyone, because he knew he deserved to be paid the same rate as everyone else.

- Hard work didn't bother Granddaddy. He knew that the more hard work you do, the easier it gets.

- Every time Granddaddy offered a little enlightenment to those who were stumbling in the dark, he gained clarity about his own values and morality.

- Granddaddy gave a helping hand to those who were less fortunate, he earned the satisfaction of repairing some of the hurt in the world, and went away feeling even more grateful for his own blessings.

Granddaddy was right about so many things. It's not a good lesson unless it teaches you how to be more truly yourself. It's not what you know, and certainly not *who* you know. Its who and what you *are* that count. His message was simple: *change your life by changing your mind.* You don't have to look like, act like, or be like anybody else; you are good enough just as you are. All you need to do is come into your own, real "being."

Many times, when we would sit for hours on the banks of muddy Arkansas lakes and fish together, Granddaddy played the mirror game with me. He would ask me to look down into the water and tell him what I saw. "Me," I would always say. Then he'd ask, "How do you see yourself five years from now? How about ten years from now?" I replied that I wanted to go to high school and have a big house and a fast car. "By hammers, son, don't just look at what you want to *have* and *do.* Look at what you'll have to *become!* All that other stuff follows if you're being the right person."

Granddaddy taught me that everything I believed to be real was just a matter of perception. Life is built on attitudes and beliefs, which have a powerful effect on perceptions. When you change your mind, when you change what you believe to be true, you automatically change what you perceive. Because of Granddaddy, I learned that I could do whatever I set out to do and be whoever I wanted to be. I believed so much in what he helped me to see that, later in life, when people told me differently, I didn't trouble myself. I just knew they were mistaken.

Granddaddy taught me to live based on what I see in my own mirror, not the distorted mirrors that others may hold up for me. I believe in my own freedom and sovereignty, and am limited only by the borders of my own beliefs. That is what I live by; that is what I teach others.

I am grateful, every day of my life, for General Cook, my Granddaddy, and the possibilities that he unlocked in me. No sticky spot in the "Barbed Wire" fence of life will ever stop me. I use the skills he taught me to get back to the "smooth" part of life.

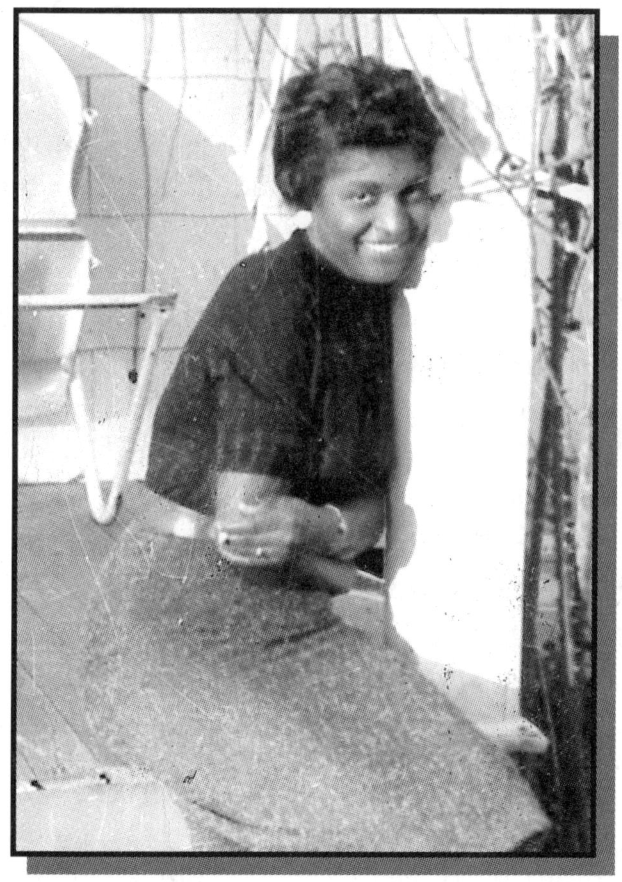

Mellonie Cook "Momma"

About the Author

Greg Winston is a pioneer in the study of high performance in the area of sales. Since he founded Sales2saleS.com in 1999 his innovative ideas and methods have had a lasting positive impact on the careers of hundreds of marketing professionals. Companies at all levels use his seminars and training programs with proven tools for increased personal and professional success. Local and national sales teams use the **Authenticity Zone** concept that Greg originated. His talents for enhancing motivation and achievement keeps him busy speaking to company and association meetings. Greg is one of the few speakers guaranteed to receive a standing ovation.

In his early years Greg began a sales career with the Xerox Corporation and became one of their lead sales professionals. At one point his year-to-date sales figures were 10 times more than the average sales representatives. While most sales representatives averaged 125% of budget, Winston set a branch record of 1003%. Immediately following that success he was then promoted to work with new hires. He used those same concepts during stints with CBS Television and Radio then Warner Bros.

In leisure hours his hobbies are reading, working out, computers and shopping too much. Greg makes his home in Seattle, Washington and his family resides in Arkansas, Illinois, California and New York.

Quick Order Form

E-mail: gwinston@Sales2saleS.com

Call: (206) 706-5191

Write: Greg Winston, 300 Queen Anne Ave., Ste. 339
Seattle, Washington 98109

❑ Please send me _____ copies of ***When Life Is A Barbed Wire Fence*** at $19.95 each, plus shipping and handling.

Name: ______________________________ Date: _________

Address: ____

City: __________________ State: _______ Zip: __________

Phone: ____

Email address: _______________________________________

Sales tax: Please add 8.7% for products shipped to Washington addresses.

Shipping: US: $4 for the first book and $2 for each additional book.
International: Based on ship-to location and current rates; please call for exact amounts.

Payment type: ❑ Check / Money Order enclosed ❑ Credit card

❑ Visa ❑ Mastercard ❑ American Express

Credit card #: _______________________________________

Name on card: ______________________ exp date: ____ / ___

Signature: ____

To contact Greg for motivational speaking, consulting, or other products

Call: (206) 706-5191,
E-mail: gwinston@Sales2saleS.com
Visit his Web site at: www.Sales2saleS.com